There are seven types of sea turtles.

A tiger pistol shrimp's snapping claw is louder than a jet engine.

Great white sharks can smell blood from 5 kilometres (3 miles) away.

A SEAL'S WHISKERS CAN SENSE A FISH SWIMMING 183 METRES (600 FEET) AWAY.

Just call me MR SENSITIVE.

A VIPERFISH HAS FANGS SO LONG THAT THEY DON'T FIT IN ITS MOUTH.

ONE TYPE OF DEEP-SEA SQUID HAS LIPS THAT LOOK LIKE HUMAN TEETH.

ELECTRIC EELS create up to **600 VOLTS** of electricity – enough to shock a person to death!

The snapping shrimp uses one of its claws as a **WATER PISTOL.**

A mantis shrimp can punch with the force of a moving bullet.

THE LARGEST FISH IN THE SEA, THE WHALE SHARK, IS LONGER THAN A BUS.

A bull shark can weigh almost as much as a **grand piano.**

2 METRES (6 FEET) : THE HEIGHT OF A MALE ORCA'S DORSAL FIN

The ocean sunfish can weigh up to 2,300 kilograms (5,000 pounds).

The Japanese spider crab can measure 4 metres (12 feet) from claw to claw!

SNAKEHEAD FISH CAN SURVIVE OUT OF WATER FOR UP TO FOUR DAYS.

DOLPHINS

work together to bring an injured dolphin to the surface of the water to BREATHE.

Hagfish tie themselves in knots to keep from being eaten.

If an OCTOPUS loses an arm, a new one grows.

Pretty **HANDY**, eh?

SEA CREATURES THAT CAN CHANGE THEIR GENDER:

anemone fish

parrotfish

hawkfish

A sperm whale can hold its breath for up to **90 MINUTES.**

A sperm whale eats about a **TONNE** of squid, octopuses and fish in a single day!

THERE IS ONE TYPE OF ICEFISH THAT HAS CLEAR BLOOD.

STARFISH HAVE NO BLOOD.

Who needs **BLOOD**, anyway?

Octopuses, lobsters and squid have blue blood.

A colossal squid's eye is the size of a **DINNER PLATE.**

SHARKS DON'T BLINK.

SOME LOBSTERS ARE COMPLETELY BLIND.

23

THE PEANUT WORM CAN PULL ITS HEAD (INCLUDING TENTACLES) INSIDE ITS BODY.

A sun jellyfish has poisonous tentacles that are more than **60 metres (200 feet) long.**

Sea lions have excellent eyesight. Some countries have trained sea lions to find equipment lost at sea.

Humans have trained **DOLPHINS** to use sonar to find **UNDERWATER MINES.**

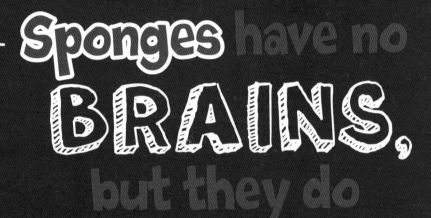

Sponges have no **BRAINS,** but they do **sneeze,** and one sneeze can last for **ONE HOUR!**

Firefly squid have hundreds of **blue** flashing lights.

DEEP-SEA DRAGONFISH WAVE AROUND A LIGHTED BARBEL TO ATTRACT FOOD.

Lantern sharks glow in the DARK.

WHOSE HEARTBEAT?

A blue whale's heart beats only 8–10 times per minute.

MANATEES: 40-80 BEATS PER MINUTE

Antarctic fur seals: 110 beats per minute

SHARKS ARE OLDER THAN DINOSAURS!

Scientists think coelacanths have been around for **300 MILLION YEARS.**

FLYING FISH USE THEIR DORSAL FINS TO GLIDE THROUGH THE AIR.

Great white sharks can launch themselves 2–3 metres (8–10 feet) into the air.

WHAT IS IT?

A **MIMIC OCTOPUS** CAN CHANGE ITS SHAPE AND COLOUR TO LOOK LIKE A **LION FISH!**

A vampire squid has red eyes.

Some see-through shrimp attach themselves to see-through jellyfish.

The glass squid is covered in polka dots.

The barrelfish
has a see-through
HEAD.

Pink handfish use their front fins to walk on the sea floor.

The tripod fish props itself up on two fins to stand on the sea floor.

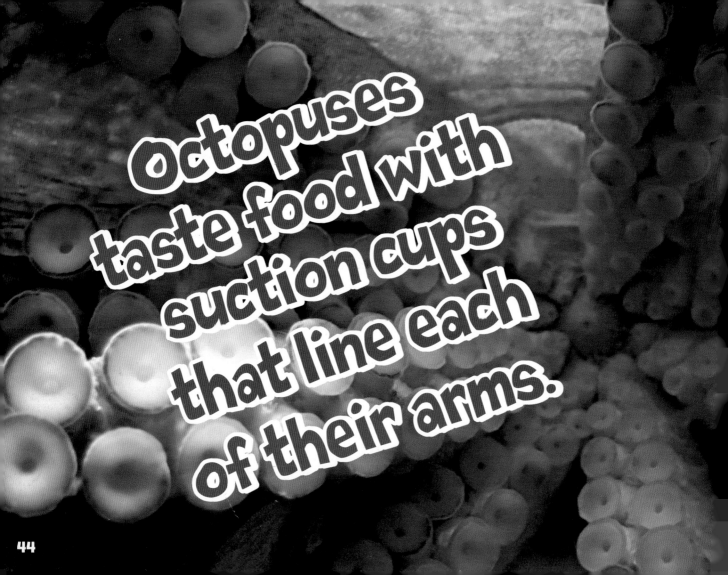

Octopuses taste food with suction cups that line each of their arms.

An octopus
can
squeeze
through
any opening
that's bigger
than its beak!

A blue whale is about 8 metres (25 feet) long when it's born.

That's almost the length of TWO CARS!

1 JELLY BEAN= the size of a newborn sea horse

Please don't EAT me!

47

Some sea cucumbers look like **poo.**

Cleaner wrasses eat **infections** off of other fish.

HUMANS USE OILY LUMPS FROM A WHALE'S STOMACH TO MAKE PERFUME.

THINGS THAT HAVE BEEN FOUND IN SHARKS' STOMACHS:

human limbs

wine bottle

50

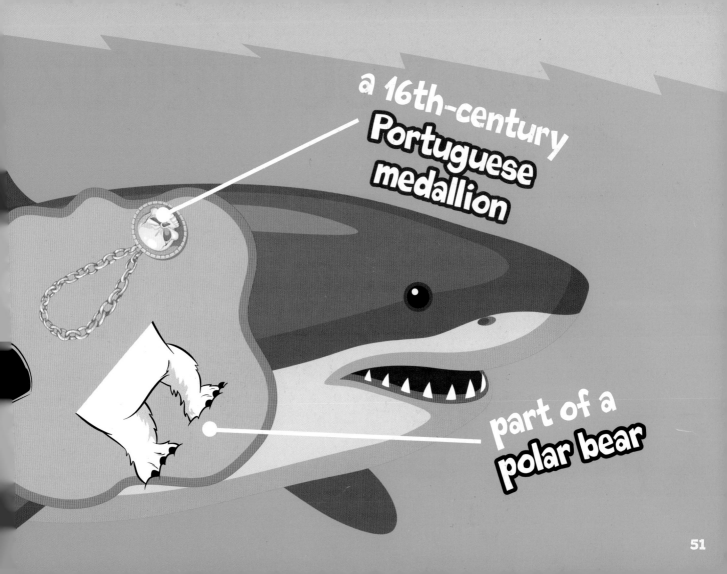

a 16th-century
Portuguese
medallion

part of a
polar bear

DO YOU THINK

Jellyfish are actually MARINE COELENTERATES.

THESE ARE FISH?

Starfish are really **MARINE ECHINODERMS.**

When a **colossal squid** swallows prey, the food enters its **brain** before its **stomach.**

A WALRUS' MATING CALL SOUNDS LIKE A BELL RINGING.

The oyster toadfish sounds like A FOGHORN.

Penguins **SING** to each other.

Walruses turn PINK when they get really HOT.

HUMANS turn pink too!

Cuttlefish can change colour to match their surroundings.

Sea otters HOLD HANDS while sleeping.

ORCAS slap the surface of the water to make waves that push animals off the ice. Then the orcas feast!

AN ORCA IS SOMETIMES CALLED A KILLER WHALE, BUT IT'S ACTUALLY A LARGE DOLPHIN.

AN ORCA DOESN'T CHEW ITS FOOD.

A MANATEE'S INTESTINES CAN BE AS LONG AS THREE AND A HALF BUSES!

The poison in one pufferfish can kill 30 humans.

A FEW MINUTES: THE TIME IT TAKES FOR THE TOXINS FROM A BLUE-RINGED OCTOPUS TO KILL A HUMAN

Parrotfish eat coral and poo SAND.

One parrotfish poos about 100 kilograms (220 pounds) of sand per year.

SEA FLATWORMS POO OUT OF THEIR MOUTHS.

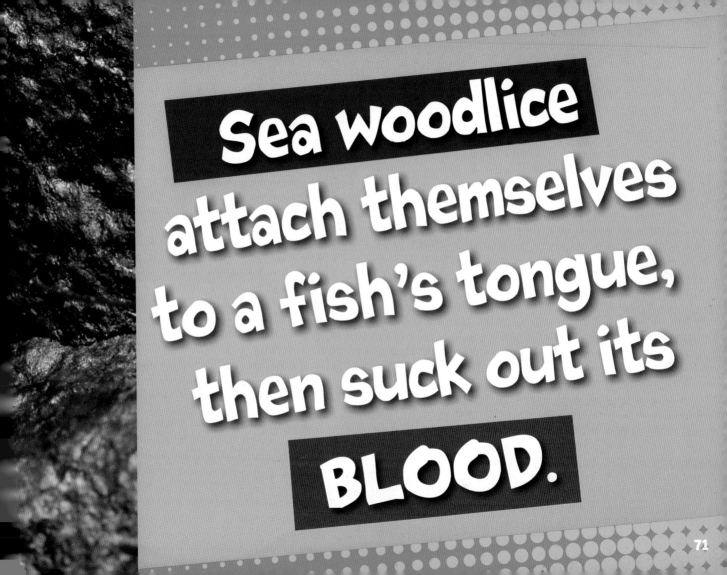

Sea woodlice attach themselves to a fish's tongue, then suck out its BLOOD.

A great white shark has about 300 teeth!

A DRAGONFISH HAS TEETH ON ITS TONGUE.

A dolphin's tooth has
growth rings
that show its age.

A NARWHAL'S
TUSK IS REALLY A
TOOTH THAT GROWS
THROUGH ITS LIP.

Can I **SLEEP** now?

A POLAR BEAR ONCE SWAM FOR NINE DAYS BECAUSE IT COULD NOT FIND AN ICE FLOE TO REST ON.

Sea turtles lay their eggs on the same beach where they hatched.

Humpback whales travel more than 16,000 kilometres (10,000 miles) in one year.

75

A clingfish uses its pelvic fins to stay attached to rocks in crashing waves.

SLEEPER SHARKS

SUCK UP FOOD FROM THE SEA FLOOR LIKE A VACUUM CLEANER.

A leafy
sea dragon's
slurping snout
sucks up
SEA LICE.

YUM!

A SCHOOL OF HERRING CAN INCLUDE TENS OF MILLIONS OF FISH.

The largest starfish is 60 centimetres (2 feet) across. The smallest starfish is about 1.3 centimetres (½ inch) across.

When a starfish eats, its STOMACH pops out of its body!

SOME STARFISH HAVE 40 ARMS.

SOME STARFISH EAT WHATEVER THEY CAN FIND – EVEN DEAD PENGUINS.

A blue whale **EATS** 40 million krill in one day.

A great white shark can eat a seal in 10 bites!

A SPERM WHALE EATS ABOUT 20,000 SQUID IN ONE WEEK.

Scientists have seen the **FRILLED SHARK** only a handful of times.

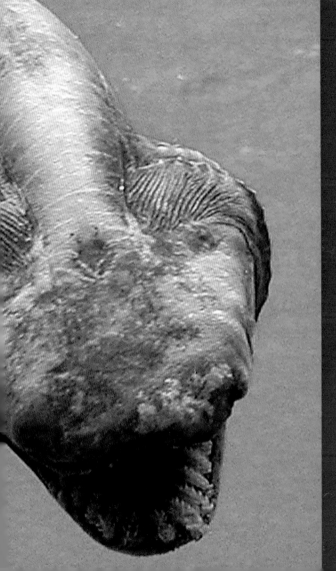

NO ONE HAS EVER SEEN A GIANT SQUID EAT.

WOULD YOU EAT THESE FOODS?

- ☑ calamari (squid)

- ☑ fizzy drink made from eel parts

- ☑ tuna eyeballs

Humans eat dried sea cucumber powder to ease joint pain.

The venom in a **box jellyfish** can stop a human heart in just ➤ *30* ➤ SECONDS!

A GIANT OCTOPUS CAN DROWN AN ADULT HUMAN.

Giant clams have been known to snap shut on PEOPLE'S HANDS.

SHARKS ATTACK FEWER THAN 100 HUMANS PER YEAR.

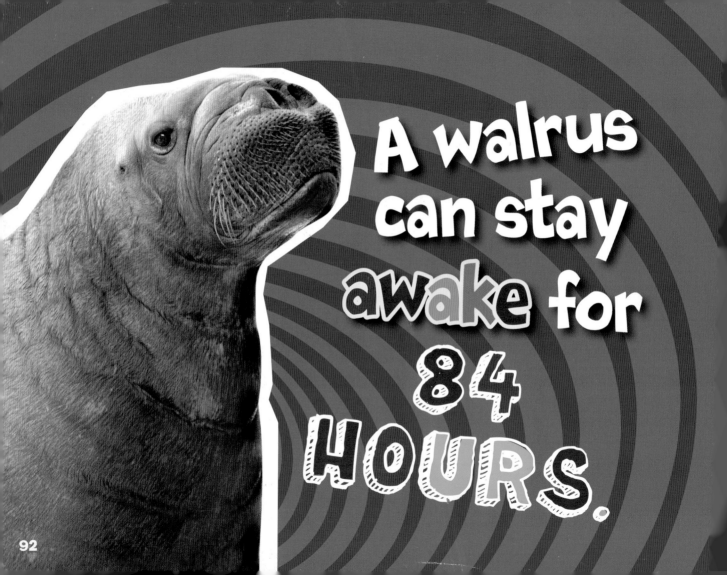

A walrus can stay awake for 84 HOURS.

Dolphins sleep with one eye open.

SOME SEALS NAP USING HALF OF THEIR HEAD AND ONE FLIPPER TO STEER.

LOOKING FOR SOME COLOURFUL CREATURES?

parrotfish

sea anemone

LOOK AT THIS LOT!

Christmas tree worms

sea slug

MANTA RAYS DO SOMERSAULTS.

Dolphins throw jellyfish into the air with their heads.

Orcas **PLAY** with their food.

SHARKS HAVE NO BONES. THEY HAVE CARTILAGE.

But I'm one **TOUGH** fish!

SHARKS SINK IF THEY STOP SWIMMING.

HUMANS ARE A SHARK'S WORST ENEMY.

Relative to body size, a fangtooth fish has the largest teeth of any sea animal.

A walrus' teeth can break through 20 centimetres (8 inches) of ICE.

The stargazer fish can give passing creatures an electric shock.

103

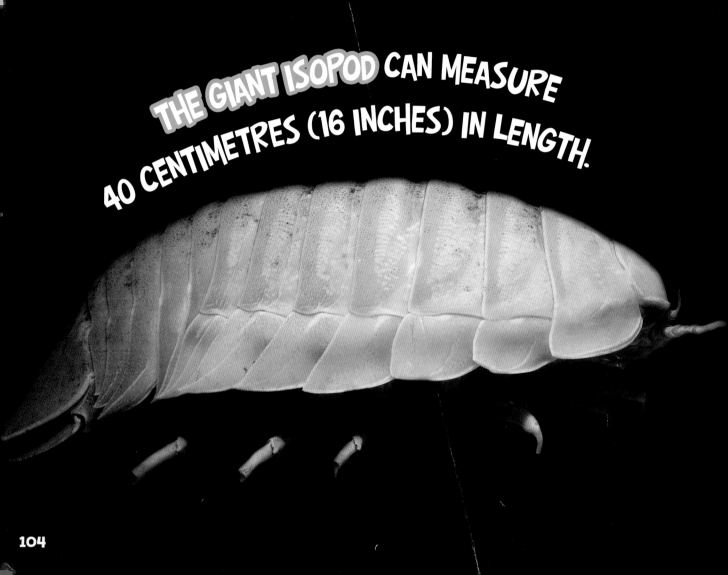

THE GIANT ISOPOD CAN MEASURE 40 CENTIMETRES (16 INCHES) IN LENGTH.

GIANT TUBEWORMS

grow to be 2 metres (7 feet) long!

Some anglerfish are the size of a 3-year-old child.

A dumbo octopus can live at depths of 4,000 metres (13,000 feet).

Despite its GIGANTIC size, the basking shark eats tiny plankton.

GLOSSARY

attract pull something towards something else

barbel whisker-like feeler on the heads of some fish

cartilage strong, rubbery tissue that connects bones in animals

dorsal fin fin on the back of a fish's body

gender being male or female

ice floe sheet of floating ice

infection illness caused by germs such as bacteria or viruses

intestine long tube that carries and digests food and stores waste products

isopod animal that has seven pairs of legs, three main body parts and a hard outer shell

krill small, shrimp-like animal

medallion piece of jewellery shaped like a medal

mine small explosive device buried in water or in the ground that is set off when a person steps on it or a vehicle moves over it

pelvic fin each of a pair of fins on the underside of a fish's body

plankton tiny plants and animals that drift in the sea

tentacle long, arm-like body part that some animals use to touch, grab or smell

READ MORE

Animal Infographics (Infographics), Chris Oxlade (Raintree, 2015)

Fantastic Fish (Extreme Animals), Isabel Thomas (Raintree, 2012)

SuperNature (DK Nature), Derek Harvey (Dorling Kindersley, 2012)

WEBSITES

www.bbc.co.uk/nature/collections/p00hldcc
Discover facts about nature's record breakers.

www.guinnessworldrecords.com
Learn about interesting world records and watch amazing video clips.

INDEX

anemone fish 16

anglerfish 106

barrelfish 41

blobfish 49

Christmas tree
   worms 95

clams 91

cleaner wrasses
   48

clingfish 76

coelacanths 35

cuttlefish 59

dolphins 14, 27,
   63, 73, 93, 96

dragonfish 31, 72

eels 8, 87

fangtooth
   fish 100

flying fish 36

giant tubeworms
   104, 105

hagfish 14

hawkfish 17

herring 79

icefish 20

isopods 104

jellyfish 25, 40,
   52, 90, 96

lobsters 21, 23

manatees 33, 64

manta rays 96

narwhals 73

octopuses 15, 19,
   21, 38, 44–45,
   67, 91, 107

orcas 11,
   62–63, 97

oyster toadfish 56

parrotfish 17,
   68, 94

peanut worms 24

penguins 57, 81

pink handfish 42

polar bears
   51, 74

pufferfish 66

sea anemone 94

sea cucumbers
   48, 88

sea dragons 77

sea flatworms 69

sea horses 47

sea lions 26

seals 5, 33, 93

sea otters 61

sea slugs 95

sea turtles 3, 75

sea woodlice 71

sharks 4, 10, 11,
   23, 31, 35, 37,
   50–51, 72, 76,
   82, 84, 91,
   98–99, 109

shrimp 4, 8, 9, 40

snakehead
   fish 14

spider crabs 13

sponges 29

squid 7, 19, 21,
   22, 30, 39, 40,
   55, 83, 85, 87

starfish 53, 80–81

stargazer fish 102

stingrays 2

sunfish 11

tripod fish 43

tuna 23, 87

viperfish 6

walruses 56, 58,
   92, 101

whales 18–19, 32,
   46, 48, 75, 82,
   83

Raintree is an imprint of Capstone Global Library Limited, a company incorporated in England and Wales having its registered office at 7 Pilgrim Street, London, EC4V 6LB – Registered company number: 6695582

www.raintree.co.uk
myorders@raintree.co.uk

Text © Capstone Global Library Limited 2016
The moral rights of the proprietor have been asserted.

Edited by Shelly Lyons
Designed by Aruna Rangarajan
Creative Director: Nathan Gassman
Production by Lori Barbeau

ISBN 978 1 4747 0587 5 (hardback)
19 18 17 16 15
10 9 8 7 6 5 4 3 2 1

ISBN 978 1 4747 0592 9 (paperback)
20 19 18 17 16
10 9 8 7 6 5 4 3 2 1

British Library Cataloguing in Publication Data
A full catalogue record for this book is available from the British Library.

Every effort has been made to contact copyright holders of material reproduced in this book. Any omissions will be rectified in subsequent printings if notice is given to the publisher.

Printed and bound in China.

Acknowledgements
Alamy: Danté Fenolio, 104, National Geographic Image Collection, 24; Corbis: Science Faction/Norbert Wu, 41, Visuals Unlimited/David Wrobel, 6; Dreamstime: Ew Chee Guan, 70, Izanbar, 77; Getty Images: Awashima Marine Park, 84—85, Dante Fenolio, 107; Minden Pictures: Norbert Wu, 100, Tsuneo Nakamura, 30; Newscom: imagebroker/FLPA/Andrew Parkinson, 37, Photoshot/NHPA/Franco Banfi, 83, Photoshot/Oceans-Image/Linda Pitkin, 108, WENN/ZOB/CB2/Karen Gowlett-Holmes, 42, Zuma Press/Caters News/ Kerryn Parkinson, 49; Shutterstock: 578foot, 69, abracadabra, 75, Adrian Kaye, cover (top left), advent, 7, alphabetMN, 32—33, Amanda Nicholls, 28—29, Andrea Izzotti, 102—103, Apostrophe, 94—95 (back), aquapix, 94 (left), Azuzl, 51 (medallion), basel101658, 11 (left), bcampbell65, 95 (left), cbpix, 17 (left), 98—99, Christian Musat, 62—63, dedMazay, 8, 96, Dominique de La Croix, 72, Elena Yakusheva, 92, Ethan Daniels, 67, ForeverDesigns, 23 (right), Fractalgr, 86, Fred Goldstein, 60—61, Giovanni de Reus, 51 (polar bear), Grigory Kubatyan, back cover, 57, Hal Brindley, 58, Ilya D. Gridnev, 44—45, Jiri Vaclavek, 52, Jiripravda, 76, John A. Anderson, 9, Kitch Bain, 47 (inset), Leonardo Gonzalez, 78—79, littlesam, 95 (right), lkeskinen, 46, Lonely, 39, Mana Photo, 15, mary416, 88—89, Matt Knoth, 53, Memo Angeles, 50 (body parts), mhatzapa, 50 (bottle), Michael Rosskothen, 82, nitrogenic, cover (top right), orlandin, 38, PandaVector, 43, Phu Hong Phu, 91 (left), pichayasri, 68 (bottom), pnDl, 19, Polly Dawson, 3, pukach, 48, R. Gino Santa Maria, 90, ra2studio, 91 (right), Rich Carey, cover (bottom left and right), 17 (right), 68 (top), Rozhkovs, 106 (left), Sean Pavone, 12, Sergey Skleznev, 94 (right), Shane Gross, 18, Simple Concept, 54, Sphinx Wang, 20, Spreadthesign, 50—51, Stephen Lew, 97, Stephen Rees, 56, Sylvie Bouchard, 5, Takashi Images, 16, Tania Zbrodko, 22, TashaNatasha, 25, Tobias Arhelger, 80, tororo reaction, 10, Tory Kallman, 11 (right), Valentyna Chukhlyebova, 34, 74, Wayne Johnson, 64—65, whiteisthecolor, 106 (right), Yusran Abdul Rahman, 21; SuperStock: Mark Conlin, 14, Stuart Westmorland, 47; U.S. Navy Photo by Photographers Mate 1st Class Brien Aho, 27

Design Elements by Capstone and Shutterstock

All the internet addresses (URLs) given in this book were valid at the time of going to press. However, due to the dynamic nature of the internet, some addresses may have changed, or sites may have changed or ceased to exist since publication. While the author and publisher regret any inconvenience this may cause readers, no responsibility for any such changes can be accepted by either the author or the publisher.